Praise For The Handym

MW01042677

Five Stars by Handyman

Get started in the right direction.

I researched a lot of books on this subject before I chose this one, and I'm glad I did.

A family member bought me some books on starting a business and they didn't really cover any of the information I was looking for. This business is a business however you sell yourself and your abilities, not a product made somewhere else by someone else in a rented space.

This book was informative and gave practical knowledge and experience that was easy to understand.

I would recommend this book to those who are thinking about going out on your own, and those who already have...

Four Stars by James Riley

Highly recommended

Very good reference guide for anyone considering starting a handyman business. I love doing handyman chores and am thinking of starting a part time small business when retired.

Five Stars by Jeremy

Great book written by a good man

Good useful information for anyone with a home repair business. I enjoyed the read and will use the information in my business. Thank You Bill.

Five Stars by Brian

Awesome

This book tells you everything you need to know from getting jobs to what tools you need I dont read much but this book was easy to read snd under stand great great book he tells you step by step what you need...recomd it highly.

Five Stars by G. Luckett

Excellent Guide

I have owned a handyman business for about 12 years now and found this to be a very good guide. I even got some new ideas to try.

Four Stars by Susan

Good book

the book is well thought out and answers many of the questions that one should consider when contemplating this endeavor.

Five Stars by Mike 1912

This is a great read

This book has all the information you'll need to start your own handyman business. I particularly appreciated Mr Benitez's chapter, "How Much To Charge and Why" on determining how much to charge your clients. Something many struggle with; especially those new to the business. Use Mr. Benitez's math and you'll stay in business! Check out the author's blog at woodworking-business.com/woodworkbiz/

Five Stars by PenNameWilliam

Retired Contractor with MBA uses book as checklist

Even as a retired contractor with an MBA, I found this book most helpful as a checklist of things to consider in starting my own handyman business. It is an excellent summary of what everyone should know about a small building business and about building a business. The writing style is to the point, thorough, and with no added fluff. You will learn about everything from customer service to internet marketing to business legal issues. But perhaps the most important thing I learned happened in thinking through all of the things he tells you to consider when figuring out what to charge. And he uses real numbers you can use today.......

The Handyman's Guide To Profit

Using Your Skills To Make Money

In Any Economy
Even In A Pandemic

2020 Revised Edition

A. William Benitez

The Handyman's Guide To Profit

Using Your Skills To Make Money In Any Economy Even In A Pandemic

2020 Revised Edition

A. William Benitez

Cover by A. William Benitez
Cover Photo by Barbara Frances
All Rights Reserved

Published By
Positive Imaging, LLC
http://positive-imaging.com
bill@positive-imaging.com

ISBN   9780984248001

Contents

Introduction

When I wrote the first edition of this book in 2009, the economy was in trouble and thousands of jobs in various industries were being lost everyday. Unemployment across the country had surpassed nine percent and in some communities it had passed twelve percent. Now, in 2020, the Covid-19 pandemic has caused even worse conditions for many. While the financial markets seem to have weathered the worse of it, employees in most fields are suffering as unemployment remains high while those who can work from home.

Even with the first stimulus package, unemployment compensation programs were overwhelmed with applicants for assistance surpassing records and many reaching the end of their eligibility and still unable to work.

Many took significant pay cuts but were glad to have something to pay their bills and avoid going under. Even some with jobs were losing their homes because their mortgage payments were no longer affordable. For many Americans it remains a bleak picture.

Many of these individuals have home repair (handyman) skills they could use to increase their income promptly and with little investment. Home repair and improvement was and still is a multi-billion dollar business. The Home Depots, Lowes, and other home improvement stores across the country are still a reflection of the popularity of home repair.

As I write this revision, the pandemic seems to be gaining and it's difficult to see the end. People are staying in their homes to avoid Covid and most aren't thinking about purchasing new and larger homes. This opens up a large market for anyone with home repair and home improvement skills. Some of that work involves major remodeling and is most often handled by professional home improvement contractors. But much of it involves small jobs that could form the basis of a profitable business for those with basic home repair skills.

At this writing, the average hourly rate for an self employed handyman ranges from $60 to $75, considerably higher than when this book was first written. Even though wages are still flat, home repair work is paying more now and by developing additional skills this amount can be much higher.

Homeowners everywhere are regularly making repairs and improvements to their home. Most of them will need some help at one time or another. Purchasing this book reflects your interest in helping these thousands of home and business owners across the country to get these repair jobs done well and at reasonable cost.

In this book, home repair business and handyman business are interchangeable. This business is often referred to by either name and both mean exactly the same thing. The term handyman refers to a person who performs various repair jobs on a home or office. This could be either a man or a woman. Anyone with basic home repair skills can use this book to make money and establish a financially successful small business.

If you have already been making repairs to your own home or helping out friends and family to get their home repairs done, you have the basic skills needed for this business. This book will help you expand those skills and make the best possible use of them by developing them into a profitable business.

The handyman business shows so much financial potential that there are even franchise opportunities available. Just Google handyman and check it out for yourself. Joining a franchise is certainly is one way to get started but you can do your own thing and keep much more of the profit by using the information in this book. This also allows you to control your own activities and maintain pricing at a more competitive level. Chapter One discusses the first step which is to determine if the business is for you.

Once you determine that running a part time or full time home repair business is for you, an in-depth inventory of your skills is critical. Obviously, different people have various skills and even various levels of those skills. To do the best possible work and ensure profit for yourself and the satisfaction of your customers, you need to recognize the things you do best and the weak areas where you need additional or improved skills. Chapter Two helps you discover your best skills and shows how to develop others.

Tools and Work Vehicle

Home repair requires a fair collection of tools but it's not necessary to have the more expensive commercial duty tools to get started. Your present collection of tools is probably quite adequate for most home repair work. Chapter Three will help you to make the best use of the tools you already have and explain how to make the best use of consumer level tools if you must purchase more. Chapter Four covers how to set up a work vehicle to help you be prepared for any job.

Licensing, Accounting, and Taxes

Once your inventories are complete and you feel ready to get started with the business, it's time to determine all of the licensing, accounting, and tax issues you will face. This varies greatly depending on the community where you live and the level of work you will be doing. It certainly won't be the same for someone who is doing small jobs on the weekend as for someone working the business full-time. The important thing is to get all of this worked out before contacting a single customer. Chapter Five helps you make certain to adhere to community requirements for your business. And, to make certain you meet all Internal Revenue Service tax codes, it describes the best ways to handle the necessary accounting procedures for any successful business.

Getting Started

Now you are ready to actually get started with the most important step of making your business visible to as many people as possible. To succeed businesses need customers and Chapter Six helps you to get started with basic, low-cost, marketing and advertising methods that will bring in customers promptly. It also covers the critically important topic of keeping customers. While getting new customers is important to any business, it costs much more to get new customers than to keep the ones you have. This chapter has changed considerably since 2009 because of the potential of social media and email.

Using Your Computer and The Internet

Computers are an excellent tool for managing many aspects of a small business including marketing, accounting, tax preparation, and research. Chapter Seven contains valuable information about using your computer and a list of excellent free software you can use to help run your business efficiently and effectively.

How Much To Charge

One of the most important and seemingly complex topic in any business is how much to charge. It is critical to get this right because charging too much will cause you to lose jobs and not charging enough will cause you to lose money. Either way your business will suffer. In Chapter Eight you will find a concise method to determine how much to charge with a solid secondary method to help you check your prices after carefully calculating them. This chapter also helps you determine when to raise your prices so you can always get the highest possible prices for your work.

Contracting Jobs

Some jobs will be so small that you can complete them in one to three hours and a verbal agreement between the two parties is sufficient. This is especially the case for small jobs that do not require the purchase of materials. Other jobs will be much larger and may take several days and require the purchase of various materials to complete. These are the kinds of jobs that require a contract and perhaps even drawings and specifications.

How much you get paid is important but even more critical is getting paid in full for every job. This involves knowing when a contract is necessary and how to prepare one. It also involves solid collection procedures and Chapter Nine describes exactly how to make certain you collect for every job. In addition to clear and concise instructions, this book contains the forms you need to run your business so you won't have to spend time creating your own forms. A link in this chapter takes you to a web site containing a set of ready to edit forms so all you have to do is change the business name to your own.

Getting Help

This book is based entirely on first hand experience operating one-person businesses over many years. It's best to avoid the cost and complexities of dealing with employees and payroll. Nevertheless, there may be times when you can use some help on a specific job. Chapter Ten covers how to get help without hiring full time employees and helps you avoid violating IRS regulations and running into payroll deduction or Social Security issues.

Your Skills

This book assumes that you already have a sufficiently high level of home repair skills to do various kinds of repair work in return for fair payment. No matter your skill level, there is always much to learn and you should keep an open mind and learn new things regularly to increase the kinds of work you can perform.

Safety

Chapter Eleven is probably the most critical in this entire book because it is about your safety. Power tools are inherently dangerous and can injure you if used carelessly or without full attention.

In this chapter you will find information to help you avoid injuries that can ruin your business and perhaps your entire life.

Final Notes

Chapter Twelve contains some final notes that I believe you may find helpful in operating a financially successful home repair business, part time or full time.

Throughout all the chapters are notes about personal experiences that should be helpful. These are clearly identified by being indented and in italics.

1

Is The Handyman Business For You?

Only you can answer this question and it's important to do it honestly. Are you handy around the house and able to make basic repairs without help? Do you enjoy doing these jobs or do you find it an unpleasant necessity? These questions should be answered before committing to starting a home repair business.

Another important question is whether or not this a good time to start a small home repair business? With Covid still looming, the economy continues suffering and the job market is still poor. This could be an excellent time to be a handyman. Owners are repairing their homes instead of purchasing new ones and this creates an excellent market for your home repair skills.

Self Employment?

Naturally, a home repair business is self employment and everything that applies to other small businesses must be considered. Financial success depends on your suitability for self employment. You must be a self starter and not someone who requires a boss to watch over your activities and make certain they are done properly. In a one-person business, you are the owner, manager, accountant, receptionist, salesperson, home repair expert and cleanup person. Perhaps a wife, husband, or other relative or friend can help you with some of the work, but you are responsible for everything.

You must consider that your income may come in spurts depending on the size of the jobs you accept and usually upon completion of jobs. If the weather or some other problem delays the work, the payment is also delayed. If you are too sick to work, everything stops including the income. Whenever you take a day off or go on vacation, everything comes to a halt, including the money. To have health care insurance, you must pay the full cost yourself and while the Affordable Health Care Act may be healthful, that could change at anytime.

In spite of those issues, there are ways to keep the money flowing, especially if you limit yourself to small jobs that can be completed in a short time. Often you will be doing jobs that are completed in hours instead of days and some may take only a few minutes.

The jobs you do are available because you have the skills and the willingness to use them. Customers want you to do the work because they either don't have the skills, are too busy to take on the work or some may have the time and the skills but simply want someone else do the hard work. They may hire you for very small jobs they could easily handle themselves. It's only important that they call you to do the job and that you perform the work satisfactorily so they will recommend you to others.

You are the sole contact for your customers. If you are doing a job that takes several days, expect calls at strange hours. All complaints come to you and, no matter how good you are, problems will arise and customers will call. It takes a lot of patience and understanding to deal with these problems.

Whether doing a job or dealing with problems, time is money so being well organized is essential. Not only will you be dealing with existing jobs but people will be calling you for information and quotes on new jobs. You will have to take breaks from existing jobs to handle sales calls. You have to calculate the price for jobs and work things out with the new customer before returning to complete the project you were working on. It's a lot of work and you have to do it all.

It isn't just the home repair work but also all the related business activities that must be done or shared with someone in the family. No matter whom assists with these tasks, you are responsible for everything in a one-person business.

This is an accurate picture of what it takes to run your own handyman business without hype or any of the romance sometimes associated with self-employment. It's important for you to see all the warts before jumping into this or any business.

2

Inventory of Your Skills

What kind of handyman skills do you already have? Home repair covers a great deal of work because it may involve almost any part of a home or office. Where has your experience lead you? Do you know how to repair doors? This can be lucrative work for those with door repair and installation skills.

Do you know how to make exterior wood repairs or patch roofing? Your skills could include repairing cabinets and furniture, installing moldings, painting interior and exterior walls, patching drywall and plaster, repairing wood floors, even repairing exterior walls or roofing, just to name a few. What are your specific skills?

It's best to begin your home repair business doing the work with which you have the most direct experience. This way you know exactly what you are doing on your first jobs and this helps assure customer satisfaction. If you have already been doing repair work around your own home or helping others on their home, you have a good idea regarding your strongest skills. Use that knowledge to make a list of the jobs that you consider your forte. These are the skills to market immediately.

Create a list of the kind of work you want to do, the kind that you would love to be doing. Once you have that list, determine your level of competence in those areas. If the level is high and you feel confident, add them to the previous list of skills. If not, determine the best way to master those skills so you can add them later.

The Internet is an excellent place for how-to research on specific jobs. You will find information, pictures, and drawings to help you learn. It is also useful to find a mentor who can answer your questions as they arise. The important thing is to competently handle any work that you add to your list. This is the only way to be sure that customers will be satisfied and recommend you to others. These referrals are the best advertising for your new business. People who call you based on word-of-mouth advertising are likely to hire you even if you charge more than others.

Learning and Training

If you require additional training on certain skills, practice them on your own home. This gives you a double benefit. Not only do you master skills for your customers, you also improve your home or office. You can photograph some of this practice work for use in your album and web site. Should you make a mistake, you will be learning from your experience without hurting your customers.

Develop part of your handyman business doing repairs on rental properties. This kind of work can be quite lucrative because it involves mostly small jobs that can be finished and collected for quickly. The main thing to keep in mind is that some landlords resist paying a fair amount for repair work. That is often offset because they are seldom as demanding as homeowners. You can determine if this kind of business works for you after the first couple of jobs and then decide whether the arrangement is worthwhile over the long term.

> *For several years I did repair work on hundreds of rental properties owned by one person. He initially called me from a small ad I placed in one of the weekly newspapers in my area. After I did a few jobs for him he began to call me regularly. During one year the jobs I did for him totaled over $13,000.00. I got one or two jobs a week and most of the jobs were small taking only a couple of hours. Owners of rental property are looking for reasonably priced, reliable handymen to maintain homes and apartments. If you perform well for them they call you regularly and become a steady source of income.*

Door Work

Doors create consistent problems in homes. Foundations settle and doors begin to stick at the top or the bottom. Or, the space between the door and the jamb tightens up causing the door to get stuck or perhaps it opens up and allows heat or cold to enter. The repair of these door problems can be lucrative.

Door work can include replacing doors but only if you have good skills. Installing new doors can be tricky and a lack of knowledge or carelessness can ruin a door. Don't accept the job of installing an expensive front entry door without experience. If you want to hang entry doors, start by replacing your own door. Never practice on your customers. There are several skills and tools that you need to do a good job installing a door. Door repair is another matter and can usually be handled with limited skills. Door issues are recurring and can be a source of regular income for any home repair expert.

Your Strongest Skill

What is your strongest skill and how can you take advantage of it? Answer that question and start profiting almost immediately. For example, cabinets and furniture often require repairs and with a little knowledge, the right skills, and careful work, those repairs can become a profitable part of your handyman business.

Specializing in this way won't stop you from accepting other kinds of work. Remain open to any work you can do even as you try to stick with your strong skills during the first year. This helps to maintain your comfort level while still making a good profit and learning new things. One simple rule that will help you succeed quickly is to avoid accepting any job that makes you uncomfortable because of limited skills.

Study To Keep Learning

Study home repair methods to improve your skills. Read everything you can find about home repairs and the kinds of projects that interest you. There are many excellent books on home repair and the Internet is filled with valuable information. Google.com is an excellent reference source for this purpose. When you have a question about a job, ask Google and chances are you will find valuable instructions.

Take the time to study and practice what you learn on your own home. The more varied your home repair expertise the more money you will make and the easier it will be to get customers.

What Size Jobs Should You Take?

Realistically consider your skill level and determine the size of jobs you will accept. If you are a one-person business, you should only accept jobs you can do alone. If the job seems too big, chances are it may be a problem to complete at your present skill level. Perhaps when you have acquired more experience and established a good reputation, you might consider bigger jobs.

> *I would always determine if I could do the job alone before accepting the contract. I did consider some large jobs but only when I felt confident that I could finish them within a reasonable time and without hiring help. During the first year stick to what you know you can do and then grow slowly as your skills increase.*

Know your limits and accept only the jobs that fall within your skills. This ensures peace of mind and avoids issues that could cause you to lose customers and money.

3

Inventory of Your Tools

The specific tools you need for home repairs vary depending on the jobs you plan to accept. You need a fair sized collection of tools to accept a large variety of jobs. Start by creating an inventory of the tools you already own. If you have been doing work around your own home, you may already have sufficient tools to get started.

Let's start by assuming that you will be doing basic home repairs including door work, cabinet repairs, and replacement of rotted boards. This is just an assumption and you may be doing other things or completely different things. In that case, you may need different tools. As long as you have already done the things you choose, you should be familiar with the basic tools needed and whether or not you already own them.

It's important to have all the tools needed for jobs you contract to do. Your inventory helps in determining if you have the tools needed for a specific job or if a purchase is necessary. The cost of any such purchases should be considered in pricing jobs.

To help ensure that you have everything needed to get started, this chapter includes a fairly complete list of useful equipment for a handyman.

What Tools Do You Need To Start?

What follows are three lists of tools. The first is a list of basic hand tools that should get you started. Immediately following that is a list of power tools that are useful for many jobs. Power tools make most jobs go faster and should be used whenever possible to save time and increase profit. The third list includes additional tools that can be very helpful but are not absolutely necessary when getting started.

Basic Hand Tools To Get Started

- **Hammers** – you should have several hammers including a couple of claw hammers, a small sledge hammer, and a ball peen hammer
- **Screwdrivers** – You never know what kind or size of screwdriver may be needed for a job. I suggest purchasing a fairly complete set including flat, phillips, square, and torx in various sizes.
- **Chisels** – For door work you will definitely need chisels but a small collection of four including sizes ¼ inch, ½ inch, ¾ inch, and 1 inch should be sufficient.
- **Pry Bars** – Also known as Crow Bars, may be handy when removing something as part of a repair. A large Crow Bar and a much smaller, flat pry bar are useful.
- **Nail Set** – Three sizes because these can be handy whenever it's necessary to set new or existing nails on a job.
- **Awl** – Get two of these because they are so easy to lose. Definitely a handy tool for most repair jobs.
- **Hand Saw** – At least one good, sharp handsaw because there are some things for which a power saw is not adequate.
- **Hack Saw** – For those times when cutting metal is necessary.
- **Coping Saw** – For small fine cuts that may be necessary in some repair jobs.
- **Mallets** – Various mallets are helpful when a hammer might damage surfaces.
- **Pliers** – Various size and shape pliers including needle nose.
- **Block Plane** – These small planes are useful for smoothing out edges and softening corners.
- **Jack Plane** – For smoothing out larger surfaces such as doors edges.
- **Knives** – Several utility knives with extra blades.

- **Wrenches** – Several different sizes including crescent wrenches, pipe wrenches, and perhaps one Monkey wrench.
- **Levels** – Small and large levels. One at least four feet long.
- **Squares** – A framing square and an adjustable square.
- **Tin Snips** – At least one pair.
- **Cold Chisels** – Handy for chipping cement when necessary.
- **Bolt Cutter** – One of these can come in handy for certain jobs.
- **Tape Measures** – One twelve to sixteen feet and then one at least thirty feet to measure larger areas.
- **Hatchet** – One small hatchet can be handy for certain jobs.
- **Caulking Gun** – To seal areas around windows and other surfaces.
- **Staplers** - A handy tool for many small repairs
- **Brushes** – For some touchup painting that may be required.
- **Clamps** – A few clamps to hold things together as necessary.
- **Saw Horses** – To make work easier on your back. The folding, plastic units are great for this because they are easy to carry in your vehicle.

This is a fairly complete list but there may be some things that you will have to purchase for specific jobs and you should always figure in extra funds for these surprise purchases.

The next list includes the power tools that could be critical for some home repair jobs. You may not need all of them so consider waiting until they are needed for a specific job before investing in power tools that you don't already have.

Power Tools

- **Drill and drill bits** – This is an indispensable tool for most home repair work. You need a good drill and a complete collection of drill bits including bits for wood, metal, concrete and various size hole saws.

- **Circular Saw** – This is a critical tool for many home repair jobs. You should also have accessories including a rip fence attachment and various carbide-tipped blades.
- **Router and router bits** – This is a tool that can be used for many jobs including decorative edges. You also need a small collection of carbide-tipped bits.
- **Belt Sander** – An important tool for rough sanding of surfaces. Get several sanding belts of 100 and other grits.
- **Random Orbit Sander** – This is an excellent tool for fast sanding while still maintaining a good smooth surface without swirl marks. Get several sanding disks of 100 and other grits.
- **Finishing Sander** – A handy machine for fine sanding of surfaces. Instead of purchasing full sheets of sandpaper and cutting them into four pieces, purchase the specialized sandpaper packs and save yourself time.
- **Saber Saw** – Sometimes called a jigsaw, it comes in handy for making cuts of various shapes. Get a good collection of blades for wood, metal, and plastic.
- **Spiral Cut Saw** – This is sometimes referred to as a zip saw. The bit is shaped like a drill bit and it can be used to cut out irregular shapes in many surfaces. Purchase a collection of bits.
- **Cordless Drill** – Just as handy as a regular drill but also serves as a power screwdriver. Purchase a bit holder and a collection of screwdriver bits of various kinds.
- **Electric Planer** – This is an invaluable tool for those who will be doing door work.
- **Electric Cords** – Have several length cords so you can use the one best suited to the job to avoid stumbling over excessively long cords.

You may also find a small compressor with one or more pneumatic nailers and/or staplers helpful depending on the kind of work you are doing.

In addition to the tools described above, your home repair vehicle should also contain some supplies including the following items.
- Various grits of sandpaper, sanding belts, and sanding pads.
- A can of Mineral Spirits also known as Paint Thinner.

- A can of Lacquer Thinner
- A collection of various size nails.
- A good collection of various kinds and sizes of screws.
- Tool Boxes to carry tools into the job site.
- Duct Tape

Purchasing Power Tools

You can find many of the tools you need at local home improvement stores. For trade level tools, find companies who specialize in selling quality tools to persons in the various trades. This is the best place to buy tools if your budget allows. However, don't overlook the many online stores who sell tools of all kinds. You may be able to save money by shopping for tools on the Internet.

Trade level tools are the best for the professional handyman but don't buy them if you already own consumer level tools. Until your business is thriving, use these tools with carbide-tipped blades and they will serve you well and save you an early investment.

Later, when you are ready to buy trade level tools, check out what you want at the local stores and then check the Internet to determine if there are any special prices on the specific models you want to purchase. Remember to take into account the price of shipping.

Carbide-Tipped Blades and Bits

Whether you purchase trade level or consumer level tools, invest in quality carbide tipped blades and bits. Most new power saws now bring carbide-tipped blades but these are inexpensive blades with a small number of teeth. Finer work requires a high quality blade with at least forty teeth and in many cases sixty teeth. This will give you a finer cut thereby improving the overall quality of your work. Whether purchasing power saw blades or router bits, insist on carbide-tipped edges.

While carbide-tipped blades and bits don't require sharpening often, they do eventually need sharpening. Find a company to handle this for you. It is difficult, although possible, to do a good sharpening job on carbide edges without the proper tools. Doing this well requires additional tools and a lot of time. You will probably be better off paying someone to handle this task. Keep all your blades and bits sharp and ready to use. This helps you perform quality work and avoid delays in completing jobs.

4

Home Repair Vehicle and Space

Be prepared for home repair jobs with either an outfitted pickup truck or a trailer to keep your tools readily available. This will also serve to carry any necessary material to job sites. In either case, you need to divide up the space in the work vehicle to keep tools organized and easy to find. This avoids wasting time looking for the tools needed on each job.

When I first decided to start my business, I didn't have a pickup truck nor a list of customers. I begin by taking on every home repair job I could find no matter how small. To do this work I purchased an old, low-sided trailer that resembled one of those old rental trailers that were popular many years ago. I built a waterproof top for it that opened to reveal the large interior space.

Inside I created dividers to organize my tools and the various supplies normally needed for small jobs. This old trailer served me well for almost ten years as I progressed gradually from home repair into woodworking and furniture making.

To avoid leaving the trailer parked in front of my home, I rented a small storage space and locked the trailer in that space every night. The first thing each day I would pick up the trailer and drive to my first job. If you have room in your garage, this cost can be avoided. It's best not to leave a trailer or truck full of tools parked in your driveway.

A locked storage space is more secure because out of sight is out of mind.

A Better Setup

I graduated from the trailer to a small pickup truck with a commercial aluminum camper shell that had doors on the sides for easy access to my tools. This was an improved set up and I organized the back of the truck with open-top wooden boxes to keep all my tools and supplies ready for any job. This is probably the ideal setup for a handyman. The aluminum camper also had racks to carry materials too long to fit in the bed of the truck.

Some home repair experts use large vans because of their large capacity for shelves and tools. This is a good setup because you can walk into the van and have shelves and boxes on either side to accommodate your tools. The only disadvantage is the higher fuel and maintenance costs. From that standpoint, a small pickup with an economical engine would be a better way to get started while keeping costs down.

Whether you use a trailer, a pickup truck, or a van, the important thing is to be organized so time isn't wasted searching for tools or incidental supplies like wood filler or caulking during a job. This will help you do several small jobs in one day and increase your profits. In addition to reducing profits, time wasted looking for necessary tools and supplies will frustrate you.

Your Own Garage Space

If you have a garage or storage space it could be useful for certain home repair jobs where part of the work can be done in advance. However, this is not critical and you can do all the work for most jobs on site.

If you plan to gradually move into more complex work, including building cabinets, a shop will come in handy and using your garage will save you money. Naturally, you have to consider local regulations and any deed restrictions in your subdivision. In some areas even having a small shop for personal use is discouraged because of the potential for noise. If you live in a rural area there will probably be few of these issues.

5

Licensing, Accounting, and Taxes

Whether home based, or a regular commercial establishment, the requirements for businesses vary from one community to another. It's critical to learn exactly what is required in your community before opening for business. The significant differences among communities may surprise you and could pose problems.

> *I operated my business in Tampa, Florida for many years and was required to purchase an occupational license there. In Austin there was no such requirement. As required in Florida, I did need a sales tax certificate so I could collect and pay the State sales tax. One community had a different licensing requirement while both States required a certificate for collecting sales tax.*

> *I also found out that both States collected a Tangible tax that is basically an annual tax on the value of the equipment used in your business. So, not only do you pay a sales tax when you purchase your equipment, you also pay an annual tax on the value of the equipment.*

Take the time to research any licensing and taxes that your community and State charges businesses operating within their boundaries. This will save you time and possibly fines for failure to adhere to local laws.

In some areas it is possible to operate completely under the radar and not obtain licenses or pay taxes if your business remains small and part-time but I discourage this idea. Instead, follow local regulations. It's better to become a participating member of the business community by purchasing licenses and registering as required to conduct business. This reflects professionalism to potential customers and will be essential once you advertise and your name becomes visible to the agencies involved in the licensing and taxing activities in your community.

The Internal Revenue Service

Most of us have been paying income taxes to the Internal Revenue Service for years. If you have been working for any employer of reasonable size, your income tax preparations are fairly simple because your employer deducts the taxes from your income and gives you a form annually describing exactly how much you made during the year and how much was deducted for income taxes and Social Security. This eliminates much of the complications and cost involved in preparing your annual income taxes even if filed by a income tax preparation company.

Keep Track of All Possible Deductions

When you begin your own business, in addition to your income, you must also keep track of all your costs so they can be deducted from your income. Failure to keep good records of income and expenses could create serious problems for you. Many businesses use an accounting software such as Quickbooks and it is an excellent software. The important thing with any accounting system is to keep it up to date. Falling behind and then playing catchup later is foolish and frustrating as you spend hours trying to prepare reports needed for your business.

If you intend to run a one-person business then I recommend online accounting. I use GoDaddy Online Accounting and have used it for years. This online service is inexpensive, secure, convenient, and accurate.

To use GoDaddy Online Accounting or any other online accounting service it's essential to separate personal and business accounts. You must have a business checking account and a credit card used solely for business. You also need a Credit Card Merchant Account to accept credit card payments. After many years using them, I suggest setting up your credit card processing with PayPal. A business savings account is also helpful.

Once you have all of these accounts set up you can sign up for Go-Daddy Online Accounting service and they will walk you through connecting all of the accounts to their accounting service Once this is completed, they scan your accounts daily and keep track of all income and expenses. The service is quite good at figuring out where each item should be listed but at first you will have to check to make certain everything is identified properly. Once things are identified correctly the service will handle it automatically from then on. They handle your accounting and you can print out reports at anytime to handle sales taxes, income taxes, profit and loss statements, and many others.

If you are fortunate enough to have someone such as a family member or close friend to handle these tasks, either free or at a reasonable cost, by all means take advantage of that. Just make absolutely certain that the records are always up-to-date and that you receive regular, at least monthly, reports on the status of your accounts. As owner of the business you should be aware of your financial situation at all times.

Part Time Businesses Can Use Checking Account For Accounting

If you only plan to run your handyman business on a part time basis, you can save time and money by using your checking account statements for record keeping. Do this by opening a checking account that is used only for your business activities, something you should do anyway. Never mix your business income and expenses with your personal funds because that is certain to cause problems.

Once you have your checking account open, make certain all the income from your business is deposited into that checking account. Pay all the business bills from that checking account by using checks or a debit card. If all your income and expenses are handled from that one checking account; it is easy to use the monthly statements for record keeping. For even more convenience, sign up for online banking so you can view or print everything on your account at anytime.

Each month, when you receive your statement and reconcile it, identify the purpose of every expense. For simplicity, you could create a numbering system that assigns each kind of expense a number. For example, Advertising = 1, Auto Expenses = 2, Repairs = 3, etc. Then you simply have to place the correct number next to the expense and put the statements in a folder for use at the end of the year to calculate your taxes.

Sign up for paperless banking and merely print the part of the monthly statement that you need. This will reduce the amount of paper that you must keep since banks now send a great deal of additional paper and advertisements with their statements.

Keep Clear and Concise Records

No matter what method you use to do your accounting, keep it up to date, make certain that you keep good records and receipts for all of your expenses. All your expenses and the cost of any tools you purchase are deductible from the money you make but only if you keep good records. You can deduct any rent, electricity, water, gas, phone, Internet connections, and any other expenses that are directly related to your business activities.

You can depreciate any equipment you purchase and, in most cases, deduct the full amount of such purchases during the same year of the purchase. You should make certain that you check this out with the IRS or with an accountant before completing your income tax forms for each year. If you handle your own tax preparation, Turbotax Online for small businesses will accurately calculate all this for you.

If you need invoices for your customers, it's a simple task to find a small and free invoice creation program on the Internet by doing a search on Google. You can create and process invoices using Go-

Daddy Online Accounting. I process all my invoices through Paypal.com

To identify specific invoices with deposits on your bank statement you can simply put the invoice numbers next to the deposits. Remember, this is only workable for limited earning, part time businesses.

You can also purchase simple generic invoices at any office supply place to save the cost of having custom invoices printed. However, the computer created invoices will allow you to add your business information and give a much more professional appearance and this is important for future business.

Save For Your Income Taxes

You should either arrange to pay estimated income tax every quarter on your handyman income or open a savings account to deposit a percentage of every job for paying your income taxes. If your business income becomes fairly high, the Internal Revenue Service will send you forms to accommodate payment of estimated taxes. Failure to pay these taxes will accrue penalty and interest charges. Estimated tax is a good idea because it avoids a large tax bill at the end of the year. It is basically a payroll deduction method for small businesses.

Pay Your Taxes On Time

No matter how you decide to handle your income tax obligations, make certain that you handle them by the prescribed due dates. If for some reason you are unable to pay your taxes in full by the due date, file your tax form and send in a check for as much as you can afford. You will receive a bill for the balance with penalty and interest added. If you still can't pay, contact the Internal Revenue Service and make arrangements to pay them in installments. Don't ignore them or fail to file an annual income tax form. Sooner or later they will come to get their money and the penalties and interest will be a significant amount.

Some say cash payments from customers need not be reported as income. This may seem true but could become problematic in the long run. Is it worth the risk? You may wisely realize it isn't a good idea and has the potential for serious consequences.

Businesses are required to pay income taxes on all of their income whether the income is cash, check, or credit card. Do you want to risk problems with the Internal Revenue Service? This is not the same kind of problem as when you make a mistake on your tax forms.

This could be considered tax evasion and at the very least generate heavy penalties and interest. There may also be the potential for frequent and inconvenient tax audits.

If the Internal Revenue Service decides that someone is not paying taxes on all their income, they will estimate the amount they believed was received in cash. If there are no records to counter their estimate of the cash payments, they will bill you for the taxes based on their figures.

If this happens and you are lucky, their estimate may be less than your actual cash income. On the other hand, it could easily be much more than you actually made and the tax bill, including penalties and interest, could be much more than if the income was reported correctly in the first place. I strongly suggest that you avoid facing this problem by keeping track of and reporting all your income.

Paying all of your income taxes to the Internal Revenue Service and other taxes could save you time, money, and headaches in the long run.

6

Getting Started

There are definite steps to take when starting a handyman business. After you have all the licensing and tax issues worked out and have organized your vehicle and tools to start serving customers, it's time to get people interested in your business so you can convert them into paying customers.

Look Professional

The first critical step in getting customers is to look like a real business. Even though you are a one-person business, it's still important to look professional in everything you do. Create or purchase business cards and some nice stationery. These need not be expensive but they shouldn't look cheap. Have the necessary contract documents prepared so that when you find your first customer everything is ready for business. Forms should be prepared neatly, not scribbled on scrap paper.

If you have completed work on your own home or for friends or family, take photos of the work and have a small album with the pictures to show your prospects. This album shows the quality of work that you are capable of doing. Have close-ups that reflect the details and the quality of the work.

These photographs can serve a dual purpose. Use them to create a web site so prospects can view an album of your work twenty-four hours a day. For information on how to create and host your own small business web site check out https://godaddy.com/ . There are other website companies including Wix. Check them out.

Contact me with any questions and I'll be glad to assist you in creating a simple website or blog.

Contact Everyone!

Now that you have everything in place, start contacting everyone you know, including family and friends. Contact them by phone, email, mail, text message, whatever method you believe is best for each person you are contacting. It may be best to contact them with more than one method. For some, personal contact may be best. Tell everyone exactly what you are doing and ask them to tell their family and friends about your new business. Give them extra business cards and make certain it lists your web site, email address, and phone number.

Don't make these impersonal communications. It's not a good idea to create a generic message and blast it out to everyone on your list. Instead, get their attention by sending individual emails to each person and personalize them as much as possible. A personalized email is more likely to be read by the recipient than a mass email sent to a list. It is a lot more work but more people will read it and respond and that's important to your success.

You might consider starting out with very competitive pricing to generate interest and introduce yourself to more customers who can then refer you to others. This may work especially well because word of mouth advertising is always the best way to find customers.

Advertise Carefully To Avoid Wasting Money

It is easy to over spend on advertising and get little benefit. Try to pinpoint your best prospects and how best to reach them. A good place to start is with local weekly newspapers. The ads cost much less than the daily papers and they are kept around for a whole week instead of just a day.

Keep the ads in the paper for a few weeks before deciding if they are showing results. A one-time ad will seldom generate results. The same ad over several weeks may start to generate interest from readers. Continue to run the ad as business comes in and until your backlog grows sufficiently. Include your web site address, email address, and phone number in all your ads. Make it easy to contact you.

Use the Internet

Don't overlook the Internet for advertising. Get your website or blog noticed by always mentioning it in every ad. This way, with just one long word, you put prospects in touch with your photo album and information about your business. Don't just build your website and forget it. Add to it every time you finish a job. Ask the owner for a testimonial and permission to use it on your website and your album. Also ask if you can use them as a reference whom prospects can call. This may help turn a prospect into a customer.

Remember that the emphasis of any advertising should be on the benefits to your prospect, not on you. Potential customers want to know what is in it for them. Don't tell them how wonderful you are. Instead, emphasize the valuable benefits they gain by dealing with you. Tell them how they are guaranteed a good job that will satisfy them completely for a reasonable price.

Tell them that you realize how difficult it is to live in a home while a messy job is going on so you will clean up after yourself regularly to avoid leaving a mess behind. Make a list of all these benefits and include that as part of every sales pitch, ad, web page, etc. You need to present benefits clearly so prospects will choose you over your competitors.

Give Everyone A Business Card

Have your business cards with you at all times because you never know when you will be sharing information about your business with someone. Together with your business card, have some brief information about the work you do so that you can share that with anyone in just a few seconds.

Be ready when you get the chance to make an impression. Have a thirty second spiel about the benefits of doing business with you memorized so it comes naturally anytime you are asked about your business. You never know when someone will be interested in the kind of work you do. Never pass up an opportunity to generate business.

Keeping Customers

Getting customers is important but keeping them is critical to your continued success. It can cost eight to ten times more to get a new customer than to hold on to one you already have. How do you go about keeping every customer for whom you do a job? It really isn't that difficult but it does take a little effort and an understanding of human nature.

The first step is to always treat your customers in ways that reflect how much you value their business. This has two fold benefits because in addition to the continued business from the customer, he or she will recommend your services to others. This second part is critical to your financial success and for it to happen you need a firm reputation for quality work and excellent customer service. Customers will only recommend those who have made a good impression. Mediocrity seldom merits mention.

Remember that excellence doesn't mean you never make mistakes. There is an old saying that goes, "Show me a person who never makes mistakes and I'll show you a person who isn't doing anything." If you do a lot of jobs, mistakes will occur and you will have to correct them. How you deal with these mistakes will determine whether a customer recognizes your excellence. Mistakes should be seen as opportunities to truly impress customers with your excellence. If you correct the mistake promptly and make certain your customer is not penalized because it occurred, your mistake will turn into a plus that will bring you much more work.

The most important part of dealing with mistakes is a prompt apology. Don't make excuses, apologize first and correct the problem immediately at no cost to your customer and then move on. This seems simple enough but many people seem to find admitting mistakes difficult and apologizing almost impossible. Think about the last time you received inadequate or awful customer service from a merchant. Did you hear an apology? Was the problem corrected the first time you mentioned it or even beforehand? If your experiences are like mine, hearing an apology seems so strange that you would definitely remember. Take advantage of this situation.

Begin correcting a mistake even if the customer has not noticed. Don't wait to be pressured into it. Your customer will be so surprised by the way the incident is handled that they will tell all their friends.

> *Dr. Wayne Dyer describes those who give him great service as eagles and those who care less about customer service as ducks. So when I get excellent service I tell my friends about it and inform them I found an eagle to help me when I was there. Eagles are rare and you have the opportunity to be one in your business so your customers will tell everyone about you.*

To serve your customers even better, don't be concerned about being right. If you believe, as some people do, that being right is the most important thing, your business is certain to suffer financially. When things go wrong in any business transaction, the most important thing must always be how your customer feels when the incident is concluded. Even if it is a serious mistake, if you admit it, apologize, and promptly make it good, your customer will think just as much or more of you than if the mistake had never happened. He or she will be convinced that you value their business and they can always count on you to perform honestly and give them good value. This will keep them coming back and recommending you to others. Remember that you are right if at the end of a business transaction the customer is convinced that he or she should come back to you the next time they need a similar service.

Good customer service pays off and it's the right thing to do. Put yourself in your customer's shoes before making a decision on any customer service issue. Determine how you would like to be treated if you were facing the same situation and treat your customer at least as well.

7

Using Your Computer and The Internet

In 2009, when this book was first published, a computer wasn't an essential tool for running a handyman business. Today I believe it is and it makes many tasks easier and helps you to stay in touch with all your prospects and customers. Computers can contribute to your financial success in many ways and in this chapter many of them are covered in detail.

> *Because I am a PC user, I have limited the information related to computer use to the work that can be done with and the software available for a PC computer. However, anything that can be done with a PC can also be done with a Mac. It's just a matter of finding the right software. Those using Mac computers may already know what software to use or will have to use Google, Yahoo, or other search tool to get information about the best programs for their Macs.*

Business Accounting and Income Tax Preparation

Your computer is the perfect tool for doing all your business accounting. In 2009 I advised starting out by downloading the free version of Quickbooks Simple Accounting. This program was adequate for most one-person businesses and could be upgraded to a full business application for a reasonable cost at a later date.

Now things are different and I don't believe this free version is even available. The trend seems to be toward online accounting which I have been doing for more than five years. The company I started with was purchased by GoDaddy and I have remained with them for several years. I have no financial interest in GoDaddy Online Accounting but I do recommend them based on my personal experience. For only ten dollars a month they will do an excellent job of handling your one-person business accounting, including invoicing. Quickbooks also has reasonable online accounting services and they are a professional and reputable company also.

Your computer is also excellent for the preparation of your income tax forms. There are many income tax preparation applications available but for me the easiest to use and most helpful is Turbotax Online. With an Internet connection you can go online and do all your taxes using an easy to follow interview process that virtually ensures you will do your taxes correctly and get every deduction you have coming. You can go to Turbotax Online at:

https://turbotax.com

> *NOTE: Since this is a paperback book, these links are not usable and you must type them into the address bar of your web browser (Internet Explorer, Firefox, Etc.). Should you experience problems please email me at bill@positive-imaging.com and I will assist you with an email link in reply.*

Photo Album and Web Site Creation

Either the iPhone or an Android Smartphone will work great to get job photos. You can save them or send them to your computer to use on your website. Create pictures at anytime and immediately after completing an impressive job. Simply edit and make only the pictures you need.

Use the same pictures to create your own web site on GoDaddy or Wix without the need for any additional software for your computer.

Here are a few things to remember when creating your own web site.

1. Resize all your photos for display on a monitor or phone display. Photo files can be quite large because they are intended for high print quality. Monitors are not capable of taking advantage of this quality so the detail is wasted. Worse yet, large files take longer to open and that means your potential customer will be waiting to see your pictures. Considering our short attention span, someone is likely to click away from your site if it takes too long to open. Resizing the pictures for the web will avoid this issue.

2. Remember that the content of your web site should be about the benefits to the customer. A little information about you is fine so customers can get to know you but the emphasis must be on what's in it for them. What will they get from you that they won't get from your competitors?

3. Create a clean, professional looking web site. It should be easy to read and have lots of white space. Tell your story in brief headings for those readers who like to click through a site. That way they will get what they need and those who want to know more can get complete information. Take the time to describe the various kinds of work that you accept and provide in depth details of any specialties. Anyone willing to take the time should be able to learn a great deal about how you can assist them to get their job completed promptly, competently and reliably.

Blogs

You should consider creating a blog instead of a website because are much easier to create, maintain, and change. They are also interactive so customers and prospects can communicate with you.

Smartphones

When this book was first published the smartphone was in infancy but now it is in everyone's hands and makes an excellent display album for all of your work. You can have an entire gallery of photos of your work and handheld access to your web site. Take full advantage of it but don't overlook the previous information as there are still people without smartphones.

Keeping In Touch With Prospects and Customers

Your computer can be invaluable for staying in touch with your customers and those prospects who may become customers. Email is an excellent tool for maintaining a close relationship with those interested in your business. However, make certain that you don't spam because it turns people off instead of creating potential customers. Get permission to send emails by placing forms on your web site or by simply asking people you meet if you can send them information.

Many large and small businesses use local email clients such as Outlook. There are many ways to handle your email, and you may already have a setup that works well for you. If not, I believe the simplest email setup is available from Google. Their email includes an excellent calendar and many other amenities that are easy and free to set up and use. Unless you already have something better, I suggest using a Gmail account for all your business email.

The important thing with email is to have access from any location. If you are using an email client like Outlook, then it should be connected with a Windows Live or Hotmail account that facilitates getting your email when you're away from your home or office.

Texting with smartphones is also a popular way for many businesses to communicate. Texting may work for you. I make limited use of texting because I dislike the tiny keyboard but that's just me.

Backup Your Computer

If you plan to use your computer for business purposes it's essential to develop a backup plan to ensure that you won't lose any of your accounting or other business information. A simple backup plan will ensure that you will have all your data in a safe location and ready to use if your computer develops issues or when you to purchase a new one.

The simplest way to backup the files on your computer is with an external hard drive. I suggest you purchase one that uses a laptop hard drive because they are compact and easy to carry with you as necessary. As you plan your backup program remember that the word backup implies two copies. Many people believe that they are backing files up because they use an external hard drive or flash drive for their files. To be a backup, there has to be one copy on the hard drive of your computer and a second backup copy on an external drive.

> *My computer is a critical tool for all my business activities. I use it for accounting, creating web sites, laying out books for publishing, editing photographs, preparing illustrations, marketing, and email. I strongly suggest that you take full advantage of how much help a computer can be in all your business activities.*

If you are not certain that maintaining a backup will work for you I suggest contracting with an online backup company. I have used Backblaze for several years and recommend them at http://backblaze.com. For sixty dollars a year they will backup unlimited data on your computer and any external drives.

8

How Much To Charge and Why

Setting the right price for every job is important and sometimes difficult because of the many variables encountered. You have to set prices that are accurate in two ways. Firstly, the price for a job must be low enough to ensure that you are competitive and secondly, it must be high enough to ensure that your business activities are profitable.

There are concise methods for calculating the price of any job regardless of the complexity but starting out it may be best to leave the really complex jobs to more experienced individuals. Getting in over your head before gaining sufficient experience can be a costly mistake. Once you decide that a job is within the realm of your skills, there are many considerations depending on the kind of job and the specific customer.

How Much Do You Want To Make?

Start by asking yourself, "How much do I want to get paid for my time?" This is an hourly figure that you apply to all jobs except when faced with extraordinary circumstances that will be covered later. This figure should be the amount you want to get paid before taxes and not including any other expenses. Do not consider materials or any overhead costs at this point.

Getting paid for your time is critical. I have run into self-employed persons who tell me how much profit they made on a specific job and I notice that the profit is quite high relative to the price of the job. As I begin to ask questions it becomes clear that they aren't really talking about profit. Their version of profit is the amount left over after paying for the materials. When I ask how much they paid themselves, they indicate that the profit is their payment. This is not the way to run a business. Profit is the amount left over after deducting all costs for the job including labor. In a one-person business the labor cost is the amount that you pay yourself. If you do not pay yourself, than the difference between the total price of the job and the cost of materials, is not accurately described as profit.

Once you determine how much you want to make for every hour of your time, consider that as part of the labor cost on every job.

The Hourly Figure

In establishing an hourly figure to pay yourself, try to balance reality with desire. Obviously, you want to get paid as much as possible for your time but you must balance the amount with what is possible in relation to the market in your area.

In 2009 a report on CNN News mentioned that handyman income was averaging $17.40 per hour. Since this was an average based on some research, it called for using a slightly higher figure of $20.00 per hour as a starting point to develop some helpful calculations. In 2017 we should consider that over eight years have gone by and the rate should be much higher. On the other hand, we have to consider that wages have remain flat because of the economic turmoil the country has suffered. I suggest you do a little research in your area to determine how much is being charged.

Remember that the figures you hear may include more than pure labor and what you are trying to establish is a price solely for your labor. You may be able to get much more and it could also be too high. You must decide the hourly figure for your job costs calculations. Make it more or less depending on what you feel is right. As long as you are being realistic, there is no wrong answer.

The other thing you must establish is the number of hours you will be working each month. In the interest of simplicity, start with

160 hours. This is basically four 40 hour weeks per month or 48 weeks per year. This leaves four weeks that you may not be able to work because of illness, vacation, etc.

This doesn't mean that you will be working this exact number of hours each month. Initially, you may be working much more. This provides a basis for the formula to be used in establishing prices for your work. In Austin, Texas the rate seems to be from $35.00 to $80 per hour for labor only with $55.00 as an average. Spend some time calculating what will work best in your community.

Buying and Maintaining Your Tools

The next item to consider is the cost of your tools. You either already have or must acquire a fair collection of home repair tools for this business. I covered the list completely in Chapter Three and you may already have most of the tools needed. Whether you already have or must buy all or part of the tools, an investment has been made and must be considered as part of your costs. In addition, they must be maintained in good working order. Over the years they may require replacement either because they break down or in order to get newer, more efficient models.

All of these costs must be considered if you expect to profit as a handyman. The process of equipment aging and requiring replacement is called depreciation. You must establish a depreciation schedule for all your tools and deposit funds into an account in order to pay for new equipment when an older piece of equipment requires replacement.

In addition to funding the replacement of the tools, you depreciate tools for income tax purposes so you can deduct these costs from your gross income thereby reducing your taxes. Even after a tool has been depreciated completely for income tax purposes, the depreciation schedule should continue to ensure that funds are deposited to be available for the eventual replacement of tools.

The easiest way to do this involves establishing an annual depreciation figure based on the total cost of your tools and the years you expect them to last. For these calculations, let's assume that the total value of your tools works out to about $4,800.00 and they are depreciated over a five year period at $960.00 per year. To calculate this you would divide $960.00 by 12 for a total of $80.00 a month for the replacement and maintenance of tools. Then divide the $80.00 by the 160-hour figure we established earlier and that would require $.50 per hour added to the hourly figure.

Work Vehicle

To handle home repair jobs you will need a work vehicle and the maintenance and fuel required to operate the vehicle. The actual cost of the vehicle is covered as depreciation just like the rest of your equipment. Let's assume that your vehicle cost $18,000.00 and you expect it to last for five years. Since automobiles have a resale value after depreciation, let's assume that at the end of five years your work vehicle will be worth $3,000.00. This leaves $15,000.00 that can be depreciated over a five year period. Divide the $15,000.00 by 60 months and then divide that sum by 160 hours. This adds a total of $1.56 per hour.

> **NOTE:** *You may be able to depreciate the full amount in the first year based on existing tax code but even if you do, it is still important to add this figure and deposit the funds because sooner or later you will need to replace the vehicle. Having the funds available will preclude the need to find financing for another vehicle.*

Maintaining and Fueling Your Vehicle

Determining your maintenance and fuel cost requires keeping good records. You can purchase a small auto maintenance and fuel journal at any office supply store to help you keep track of these expenses. Actually, in 2020 an app for your smartphone will handle this task. Let's assume that it will cost $300.00 per month to keep your vehicle properly maintained and fueled. This would add $1.88 per hour.

The High Cost of Insurance

Insurance is another high cost item that must be considered. Your vehicle requires adequate insurance to protect you and others in case of any accident, damage, or theft. Insurance coverage is legally required in most States. But this is only part of the insurance picture. Here you will have to make an important decision.

There are handymen who work without any insurance related to their jobs. This allows them to charge less for their work and sometimes save money for their customers. While this seems like a good deal for both handyman and customer, that's only the case if nothing ever goes wrong during a job.

In our litigation prone society, when something is damaged or someone is accidentally hurt, the first stop is often an attorney's office. You could wind up with a serious legal problem and costs well beyond what you can afford.

The picture isn't much better for homeowners using uninsured handymen. If you get hurt because of some unforeseen problem with the home, you may choose to take legal action against the homeowner. In that case the problem may be reversed but it's still a serious issue.

The only answer for these problems is liability insurance that covers you, your business, and your job site work. Unless you shop carefully, these insurance policies can be quite costly. This is especially so since insurance agents will try to sell you excessive amounts of insurance.

Perhaps it's true that you can never have too much coverage but it's pointless to pay so much for coverage that the cost overwhelms your business financially. I'm not an insurance expert so I suggest you contact one that you trust and make certain he or she understands that you want the minimum acceptable amount of coverage that will protect you in case of an accident. You probably won't use it but it will look good on your advertising and many homeowners won't consider using an uninsured home repair company.

The other significant consideration is health insurance. Unless your spouse is employed at a job with insurance benefits to which you can be added, you will need to purchase it yourself even though costly. This one expense alone creates many headaches for self employed persons. Even considering the Affordable Health-care Act this will be costly.

If you don't have it through a spouse, I suggest that you get at least major medical insurance coverage and keep the deductible high enough to maintain premiums at an affordable level. It is unlikely that you will be able to obtain all this insurance for less than $390 per month requiring an addition of $2.45 per hour cost.

Remember All Your Taxes

For many, federal income taxes are a nemesis. In truth, taxes are a reality you must face to do business. Unfortunately, it's not uncommon for small businesses to have problems with the Internal Revenue Service, whose job it is to collect federal income taxes. Most of the time, the problems are a direct result of failing to make adequate provisions by setting aside funds for the payment of income taxes.

Problems with the IRS can be serious and costly because failure to pay on time accrues interest and penalties that can quickly double or even triple your tax obligation.

If at all possible, pay your taxes quarterly as required by the Internal Revenue Service. If not, at least open a savings account to save a portion of your income to pay your taxes when they are due each year on April 15th. Save at least ten percent of your gross income and preferably more. Ten percent of the gross income your business receives is a significant portion but that is what is needed to ensure you can pay your income taxes on time. It is difficult to estimate the exact amount of your income taxes but you will probably pay from twenty to thirty percent of your net income.

Social Security alone comprises fifteen percent of your net income. This figure seems quite high because as a self employed person you must pay the entire cost of Social Security. Employees of a company only pay one half of the Social Security, about seven and one half percent, and the company pays the other half.

A net income of $30,000.00 per year could cost you $8,000.00 or more including Social Security and Income Taxes and this would require adding at least $4.20 per hour. This figure can vary considerably depending on your allowable deductions but it's much better to save too much than not enough. After all, it is going into your savings so whatever is left over will increase your investments or you can use it for a vacation or anything else you choose. As a final note, don't forget to save for State income taxes in those States that collect this tax.

Pay Yourself For All Your Work

As a one-person business you will be estimating every job, preparing bid presentations, picking up materials, running various errands, doing all the required accounting, and many other related tasks that consume a lot of time. To ensure a fair profit it's important to get paid for that time. It is difficult to charge customers directly for time spent on jobs before you actually get them. Therefore, you have to consider this time as part of your hourly calculations. To get paid for this time you should add at least $300 per month for an hourly amount of $1.88.

Don't Forget the Profit

There are two ways to calculate your profit on jobs. For one you can make the profit part of the hourly figure. With the other, the one I recommend, you calculate it separately based on the entire job. Either way, calculate at least twenty five percent for profit. The more popular method is to add profit based on the entire cost of the job because that allows a profit on the materials also.

You now have a basic list of all the figures necessary to calculate the price on any job. Remember, these are sample figures. You can see how the formula works but you must calculate the best figures for your area to determine the correct pricing for the labor on each job.

Check out the chart below for a breakdown of hourly charges. It calculates the hourly charge by listing all the items discussed previously. It cannot be overemphasized that the costs in your area will probably differ and you may have other priorities to consider. This chart is just an example to help in creating your own chart.

How Much To Charge Chart

Hourly Wage (You decide this amount)	$ 55.00
Tool Maintenance ($80 by 160 hours)	$ .50
Vehicle ($15,000 cost/60 months by 160)	$1.56
Vehicle Maintenance and Fuel	$1.88
Insurance ($390.00 by 160 hours)	$2.45
Taxes ($8,000/12 months by 160 hours)	$4.20
Misc. Overhead ($300 by 160 hours)	$1.88
TOTAL PER HOUR	**$ 67.47**
Profit - Hourly Basis (25% of Total Per Hour)	$ 16.87
TOTAL PER HOUR INCLUDING PROFIT	**$ 84.34**

To get started, let's round off the **Total Per Hour** figure to **$68.00** and the **Total Including Profit** figure to **$85.00** per hour.

Now let's go through a couple of sample jobs so you can see exactly how to use this information to come up with accurate pricing that will ensure you make a profit on every job.

Sample Job One

For the purposes of the first sample job, let's assume that it will take 16 hours to complete the entire job. Just multiply 16 times $85.00 for a total of $1,360.00. This is your total labor and profit on this job.

The next step is to calculate the cost of the materials. Start by using your job information to prepare a precise materials list. This list should include the quantity of each item. Strive for accuracy here because any mistakes will come right out of your pocket. Even though many home repair jobs may not be material intensive, any material costs must be accounted for or your profits will be reduced. Assign an accurate price to each item and, if in doubt, price the item higher rather then lower. You may need to contact some suppliers to get updated prices.

Let's assume the materials will cost $270.00. Add the labor cost amount of $1,360.00 to the $270.00 for materials for a total of $1,630.00, which is the total price of the job.

If you prefer to add the profit separately, use the $68.00 per hour figure times 16 and that equals $1,088.00. Then add the $270.00 for materials for a total of $1,358.00. Calculate twenty five percent of $1,358.00 and it equals $339.50. Add that to $1,358.00 for a total $1,697.50. Notice that the figures from both methods are close but the second figure is higher. You may consider this difference to your advantage on those jobs that require tighter pricing to be more competitive.

There is Always Some Waste

Remember to add a waste factor. When you are calculating jobs realize that some waste will be encountered. You will probably have to buy more material than you actually need because of this. The cost of this additional material must be covered in the job.

Sample Job Two

This time it will be a material intensive job that takes only 10 hours but requires $475.00 for the materials. Start by determining the hourly labor and related expense cost by multiplying 10 by our $85.00 per hour rate for a total of $850.00. Next, we add the cost of materials and come up with a total price for the job of $1,325.00 including profit.

Now check it using the method where we add the profit to the full amount of the job including the materials. For this we multiply 10 times $68.00 for a total labor and expense cost of $680.00. Then we add $475.00 for the materials to this for a total job cost of

$1,155.00 not including profit. Using the twenty five percent profit formula, we multiply twenty-five percent times $1,155.00 and come up with a profit amount of $288.75. We add the profit to the $1,155.00 for a total job price of $1,443.75.

Notice that this price is close but higher than the price with the profit calculated as part of the labor. Compare the two sample jobs and notice that in both sample jobs the price with the profit added separately is higher. Once again, this difference can assist you in competitive situations by providing price options that could help you get the job.

The most important thing to remember is that all of these prices would leave you a profit if your time and material cost were calculated correctly. Even though the prices are different, they would all work out fine. So, how do you decide which price to use? This requires some intuitive thinking when you are speaking with your customer.

The correct price is the one the customer is willing to pay. If it seems that the customer is ready to give you the job, go with the higher price. If you feel like the customer may be calling someone else and it may become competitive, go with the lower price to increase the odds that you will get the job.

Don't Forget The Backlog

Consider your backlog of jobs when calculating prices. If a lot of work has been coming in and you are quite busy at the time, go with the higher price. If things have been slow and you could use the work, go with the lower price. Either way, you will get paid for your time and make a profit. As time passes, your comfort level in the business increases and you become more aware of how a prospect may react to your price. This will help you decide what to do in each case.

A Final Check of Your Pricing

Since accuracy in setting prices is so important, there is a way to do one final check of your price on your first few jobs. Exactly how this check is handled depends on the complexity of the job and also on whether it is labor or material intensive.

This method should only be used to check your pricing, not to actually calculate a final job price. This is because there are too many variables involved in the process.

The first variable is to determine if the job is material intensive. For example, if the material costs comprise a large percentage of the calculations, you would use a ratio between 2.5 and 4 for your calculations. However, if the material costs are a small part of the total job, as in the job we used as the first sample, you could use a ratio as high as 6.

The second variable is complexity. If the job is relatively straightforward and you expect no major difficulties, the above ratios are fine. If the level of difficulty seems high, you could adjust the ratio by one or two before using it. Remember that this is only a backup to your normal method of calculating job prices as already described.

While this may sound complex, remember that it only serves to ease your mind about the accuracy of your pricing. You have already taken the time to properly calculate a price for the job. Once you get accustomed to pricing jobs, this final step is unnecessary.

The ratio numbers are used to multiply times the cost of materials. For example, in the first sample job the cost of materials is 270.00, the job is labor intensive, and it seems to be of average complexity so we would multiply by 6 giving a total of $1,620.00.

In the second sample job the cost of materials is $475.00, it is material intensive and the work is relatively simple so we would multiply by 3 giving a total of $1,425.00 indicating that our pricing is quite safe.

There is yet another way to take advantage of this additional information. You will run into homeowners who wish to negotiate and may make you a counter offer. With this figure in mind, you might consider accepting a counter offer close to this amount because your have tested your pricing thoroughly.

This improves your chances of getting jobs even when the homeowner considers your pricing a little high. It's not necessary to do all of these methods to establish your pricing but it allows you many options to ensure you will make money on every job.

Please remember these figures are not necessarily accurate for your area. You will have to do research to determine the prices of all items for your jobs. Determine what is considered a fair wage for the kind of work you will be doing. The cost of living in your community may be much higher and therefore the income for home repair experts may also be higher. Research this thoroughly so you don't short change yourself or overcharge and lose jobs.

The Grief Factor

You may not hear about this in any other information about the home repair business but I believe it is critically important. It was of real help to me over the many years I spent doing home repair, home remodeling, and woodworking.

As your business grows, many interesting people will be encountered. Most of them simply want a good job and as long as you deliver that everything will work out well with them. On the other hand, you will run into prospects and customers who are impossible to please and will make things miserable for you no matter how good your work. It's important to recognize and make advance adjustments for this kind of customer.

It isn't difficult to identify these potential customers and you must do it during the initial contact, before you agree to do the job. You can identify them in various ways.
- They will take an hour to explain something that most people will explain in five or ten minutes.
- They will convey all the terrible experiences they have had with other home repair companies or contractors in vivid detail.

- They will continuously repeat that they can't afford the work unless the price is extremely low.
- Even for a simple job, you will waste much more time with them than with any of your other prospects.

In short, it will be obvious that working with them will not be pleasant, hence the grief. In these situations I strongly suggest one of two methods to deal with these potential customers.

- Explain that you don't take on the specific kind of work they want done and leave as quickly as possible.
- After calculating your price, think about how much trouble they will be causing for you as the job progresses and add a substantial percentage to the price of the work.

Either of these methods will protect you. In one case, you will not have to deal with an unpleasant situation. On the other hand, if you get the job, you will get paid well for putting up with the grief. Your preference may be to leave but for enough money you might put up with a lot.

> *Years ago I spent over an hour with a potential customer and by the end of that time I knew that it would be unbearable to do the job. I couldn't say that I did not do that kind of work because they were familiar with my work. Instead, I calculated the job normally and then doubled that price. I thought the prospect was going to have a fainting spell and I did not get the job. Maybe that wasn't a nice thing to do but I have always tried to enjoy my work and it was obvious that I would not have enjoyed that job.*

You will have to make these decisions yourself and if one gets by you, it will be a valuable experience to guide you in dealing with future problem prospects.

The Rule of Supply and Demand

The rule of supply and demand is one of the most important rules of business. Small business owners often lose out on additional money they could be making for the same amount of work by overlooking this important rule. Your prices should always reflect the demand for your work. This is common practice in many businesses.

Check hotel rates during peak and slow seasons to see how they vary. You can also check airfares during various times of the year. When there is low demand, the prices go down to encourage more people to buy. When the demand is high, the prices go up to increase profits and adjust the demand to the available supply. You can take advantage of the rule of supply and demand as a one-person business. When you have a backlog of work and continue getting more jobs than you can possibly do in a reasonable amount of time, increase your prices until the work levels off to a flow rate that you can handle. The formula for how much to charge, in the previous pages, indicates pricing to ensure that you make a living. The main purpose of the formula is to make sure that you charge enough so you never lose money while making at least a small profit. It does not indicate how much you may charge for a job if it is sold to someone who knows your work and is willing to pay more to have you do their job.

The actual amount that you can charge is determined by a customer's willingness to pay, not by any formula. The right price for anything is the amount a willing buyer will pay a willing seller. Beyond that, there are no limits. Some people quarrel with this and dub it gouging. That might be the case if you are taking advantage of a desperate situation like a flood, hurricane, tornado, etc. But under normal circumstances, the market for services sets the real prices and there is no reason you should not participate in the market, even on a small scale.

It often seems that there is a preconceived notion that a self-employed person can only make wages and must be prepared to sacrifice a decent income, medical benefits and vacations to do the work he or she loves. Do you really believe that? If you do, it may well be true for you. If you know any individuals who are trying to make a living with the work they love, this may be the case for them. It doesn't have to be that way for you. If you have the skills to do a good job and charge enough for it, you can make a good living as a self-employed home repair expert.

I graduated from the home repair business into a full-time woodworking business and learned a great deal in that process. One of the truly important lessons that helped me make much more money was about perceived value and the law of supply and demand. Years ago I wrote some notes on that subject and I believe they will be helpful to anyone wishing to be in the home repair business. Those notes begin below.

NOTES ON PERCEIVED VALUE AND SUPPLY AND DEMAND

After many years in the woodworking business I learned never to limit myself by what the competition charged. As my backlog increased, I began to raise my prices and found that even people who did not know me personally were willing to pay me more for jobs because of the reputation I had developed. You may also be worth much more to your customers.

Some people are making $10.00 per hour while others make well over $100.00 per hour. There may be a significant difference in skills but what often makes the difference is the value a customer perceives. A clear example of this is the art world. One canvas may look beautiful and not be worth the cost of the canvas materials to buyers. Another canvas of the same size may look worthless to you or me and bring thousands, even millions from art lovers. This is all value perceived by the customer who is willing and able to pay the price.

The same thing is applicable to woodworkers. There are woodworkers who struggle to get a few hundred dollars for a really nice rocking chair and others who are getting thousands for a similar chair. And, the one that is getting thousands has a long waiting list. Perhaps one of those woodworkers is much more skilled than the other but more likely they are at similar skill levels. Perceived value is the key ingredient. One of the woodworkers has become famous, perhaps because of books he has written or some oth-

er public exposure. Whatever the reason, his work is perceived to have more value. Use perceived value to your advantage. If people really love your work, then charge as much as the market will bear.

If you want to be in business in a free enterprise system such as ours, you must remember that the price of everything is based on supply and demand. The maximum price of any product or service is the maximum amount that a customer is willing to pay for it. If you have a problem with the idea of perceived value and supply and demand and believe that it is somehow unfair to charge more based simply on demand, remember that this will limit your profit significantly.

Making a good living in home repair requires that you consistently charge as much as possible for all of your jobs. Considering perceived value and supply and demand will help you do that.

9

Contracting Jobs

You will need job contract forms but keep them simple because customers are hesitant to sign long, complex, difficult to understand forms written in legalese. On the other hand, your contract must protect you in the event a problem arises during a job.

Keep in mind that a good contract is an agreement between two honest people who want to do business with each other. If one or the other intends to cheat on the agreement, the contract will not resolve all issues. It may protect you to some extent but it won't stop problems from arising if you do not perform as agreed or if there is a misunderstanding between you and the owner.

This means that even with a good contract, being right is not the important thing. The most critical thing is to always complete your jobs in accordance with your agreement leaving happy and satisfied customers who will call you again and recommend you to their friends and family.

The Steps of Contracting For Work

The first critical step involves selling the customer the idea that you are the best person to do the work. Part of that will involve finding out exactly what they want and this requires listening carefully to the prospect.

Never underestimate the importance of listening. Too many people spend valuable listening time figuring out how they are going to respond. Instead, listen intently and take notes to develop a clear understanding of your prospect's desires. Once a job is clear to you, it may be necessary to prepare some simple drawings to ensure that both you and the potential customer understand what the job involves. In some cases, a simple listing of tasks is adequate. Do whatever it takes to ensure that everything is understood by both parties before calculating the cost of the job and giving the customer a firm quote or estimate.

After this is complete, if the customer decides to proceed with the work, you can prepare the contract form. The contract should define the job using the notes that you created with the prospect and should refer to any drawings, task list, or specifications prepared for the job. All of these forms should be attached to the contract form. At this point you sign the contract and give it to the customer to sign.

The Deposit

Now comes one of the most important and often overlooked part of the contracting process. Unless you are dealing with a small job that can be completed in less than one day, every contract should require a deposit payable before the work begins. Some will tell you that it is difficult, and often impossible, to get a deposit from customers. That isn't true and you will get little resistance from anyone who trusts you enough to spend the money for the job, unless they have doubts about your honesty. If such doubts exist, you are better off without the job.

Even when you are first starting, it is no problem to get a deposit as long as you present yourself professionally, carefully explain the work, present clear and concise information about the job, a fair price, and a simple contract form. When people realize that you are serious and know what you are doing, they will not resist the deposit. Once you develop a reputation it will be even easier to obtain a deposit from your customers.

As was indicated earlier, a contract with a customer is based on trust. If a customer is unwilling to sign a contract and give you a deposit, then trust doesn't exist and the customer is concerned that you will not follow through and perform as promised.

Should you proceed without the deposit, you won't be certain that you will get paid. The deposit is a compromise. The customer has a reasonable assurance that you will do the work in order to get the rest of the money. You have a reasonable assurance you will get paid the balance because the owner has contracted with you and given you a good faith deposit that he or she will not want to lose. If even this limited amount of trust doesn't exist, it is probably in your best interest, and that of your prospect, not to proceed with the job.

With home repair the amount of the deposit can vary. On jobs that don't involve materials or can be completed in less than a full day, no deposit is necessary. On larger jobs a fifty percent deposit is appropriate.

You can make exceptions for customers like rental property owners who give you work regularly and simply pay your invoices when submitted.

At a minimum, you should normally get a deposit in an amount at least equal to the cost of the materials for any job. This way, even if something does go wrong, you would not be out of pocket for the materials.

No matter the form of your contract, you will probably run into potential customers who absolutely refuse to pay a deposit. Treat the deposit requirement as standard policy that you do not bypass for anyone. I suggest you create a deposit policy covering any job that takes more than one day or cost over a certain amount. You can determine the amount you are comfortable with. Potential customers who resist the deposit may sometimes come up with various alternatives including lower percentages or depositing the money for the job in an escrow account.

It is best to reject any scenario that precludes obtaining a fair deposit before starting the work. It is also important to give deposit checks time to clear the bank before beginning the work to avoid issues with bad checks. With the speed of present electronic banking, this will seldom take more than a day or two.

On smaller jobs you can offer the customer the alternative of purchasing all the material for the job. If necessary, they can go with you to the supplier or home improvement store and pay for everything thereby precluding any financial risk on your part.

Maintaining an adequate deposit policy is the only way to make certain you do not lose money on jobs.

Credit Cards

It is simple to set up to accept credit cards and it's especially important for small jobs even though it also works for larger jobs. There are many companies with whom you can set up but I recommend PayPal with whom I have been dealing for many years. Their rates are reasonable and you only pay if you process transactions. There are no monthly minimums. Check them out at http://paypal.com .

Dealing With General Contractors

Your deposit policy will eliminate almost all general contractors as customers. There may be remodeling contractors who want to have some work done as part of a large remodeling job and they want to pay you after they get a draw from the bank financing the work. This can be a slippery slope that can cost you a lot of money.

Some contractors try to cut prices after the work is finished because they realize the remodeling job is costing more than they estimated. If you stick with your policy, only contractors who have the financial ability to pay the deposit up front will do business with you and your odds of collecting the balance when the job is done are greatly increased.

Sometimes You Don't Need A Contract or Deposit

There are some situations where a contract or deposit arrangement may not be possible or necessary. One of those involves doing work for government agencies. In those cases, it is unlikely that you will not get paid and it may not be possible for them to arrange a deposit or even sign a contract. In most cases governments work with a purchase order arrangement and you will have to accept that if you choose to do work for them.

Deposits could also be a problem when working with large corporations. They also work with purchase orders so you may have to pass on the deposit if you want their business. You should be very careful here because some people who run corporations simply don't care about their vendors and it may take a long time to finally collect for your work.

The important thing is to handle these situations carefully always making certain you collect for every job you do. If they fail to pay you for one job, for any reason, drop them immediately until you have been paid in full. This is the only way to ensure that your business will be a financial success.

Forms You Can Use

You may consider getting an attorney to prepare a simple contract but don't allow it to become a 10 to 20 page nightmare of legal jargon. This will just make it more difficult to sell jobs.

The contract and other forms you need are not difficult to create and are similar to what would be used by a woodworking business. A sample set of forms is included in this book and you can modify and use them for your home repair business. If you prefer, I also have an editable set of these forms on the web at:

http://home-repair-business.com/forms/contract.rtf

http://home-repair-business.com/forms/letterhead.rtf

http://home-repair-business.com/forms/specifications.rtf

The advantage of the .rtf forms on this web site is that you can easily edit them with your company name and address. Even though these forms have worked effectively for years, there is no legal adequacy implied or guaranteed as the author is not an attorney. Using these forms will save you the time of creating your own.

AGREEMENT FOR HOME REPAIR SERVICES   DATE:_____

This agreement is made as of the date above between **A. William Benitez,** a sole proprietor, and _____ of _____ in Austin, Texas _____, hereinafter called the **Owner.** For and in consideration of the mutual promises and covenants hereinafter set forth, the Owner and A.William Benitez agree as follows:

ARTICLE I: A. William Benitez will perform the work described herein and on any attached and signed specifications. All work shall be done in accordance with the attached drawings, specifications, and any additional notes. All work shall be completed including finishing, unless specifications specifically state that finishes are to be applied by the Owner. In such cases the work will be unfinished.

ARTICLE II: The work shall be completed as indicated above within _____ days of the execution of this agreement.

ARTICLE III: The **Owner** shall pay **A. William Benitez,** in the manner described below, the total of $_____ plus $_____ sales tax for the work listed in Article I.

Total Price of the Work…………………………………………$_____
Sales Tax……………………………………………………..$_____
Total Price Including Sales Tax………………………………..$_____
Deposit: Due Upon Execution of This Agreement…….…….$_____
Balance: Payable In Full Upon Completion of Work…...……...$_____

ARTICLE IV: Additional items of agreement: Drawings and/or specifications attached.

ARTICLE V: Miscellaneous: A. William Benitez shall furnish all materials and labor for this work unless described to the contrary in Article I or the specifications. All work shall be performed in a workmanlike manner to meet or exceed industry standards. This document and its attachments as listed in Article IV, constitute the entire agreement between the **Owner** and **A. William Benitez,** and it may be altered, amended, or repealed only by mutual agreement and a duly executed written instrument.

IN WITNESS WHEREOF, the **Owner** and **A. William Benitez** execute this Agreement as of the date stated above.

OWNER   **A. WILLIAM BENITEZ**

_____   _____
Owner   A. William Benitez

A. William Benitez Handyman Services
402 Corral Lane   447-4744   Austin, Texas 78745

DATE:_____

FOR:
ADDRESS:

The following specifications shall apply to the home repair being done for the job listed above. These specifications can only be changed by mutual written agreement of the two parties to the contract.

SPECIFICATIONS

Creative, Quality Home Repair and Prompt, Reliable Service

A. William Benitez Handyman Services

402 Corral Lane   447-4744   Austin, Texas 78745

10

Getting Help

The simplest way to operate a handyman business is by accepting only home repair that you can complete on your own as a one-person business. For me, that's always been the best choice but as business grows you may be interested in doing more and larger jobs by getting some help.

The one-person business leads to financial success with the lowest possible risk and this book is geared specifically to that form of business. There are many reasons to avoid hiring employees, not the least of which is that it could complicate your life and even take the joy out of your work.

Hiring employees also creates a significantly more complex income tax situation and employees can increase the cost of your work significantly. Obviously there will be times when you need help because you have too much work or for jobs that are too large to handle alone. Hiring subcontractors is a better way to deal with excess workloads.

Choose subcontractors carefully because they will be representing you on every job and you don't want them to harm your valuable reputation. Don't hire a subcontractor unless you are familiar with his or her work and reputation.

What Is A Subcontractor?

Using subcontractors is definitely an excellent way to handle more jobs, but make certain you avoid subverting Internal Revenue Service payroll deduction requirements by considering employees subcontractors. You can experience serious and costly issues with the Internal Revenue Service for applying the term subcontractor incorrectly in an effort to avoid employee payroll deduction and Social Security requirements.

The Internal Revenue Service has certain requirements that must be met in order to consider someone a subcontractor. Fail to meet those requirements and your "subcontractor" will be considered an employee and you will be required to pay payroll taxes and Social Security payments that you did not deduct, plus interest, and significant penalties. You can safely avoid such problems with the Internal Revenue Service by meeting certain specific standards. These standards are fairly basic and include:

- The subcontractor must have a business identity. That is, they must have an address, phone number and some past business experience with other customers.

- The subcontractor must control his or her own hours. If you have someone working for you during certain hours that you control and you pay him or her on an hourly basis, that person is an employee to the Internal Revenue Service.

Calling someone who does not meet these basic standards a subcontractor will not impress the Internal Revenue Service. If they check on you and find this kind of situation, this person will be deemed an employee and this will hurt you financially.

Day Laborers

Naturally, if you only need someone for one day to help you perform certain tasks on a specific job, you can hire a day worker and pay him or her for that day only without consequence. However, if you need help everyday, make certain that the persons who help you can be legally considered subcontractors.

In most communities there are places to pick up day laborers and this will usually work out fine. However, if you know someone or, if your handyman business is part time, you may find a friend or coworker to assist you.

This creates a more comfortable work environment and you can confidently leave someone at a customer's home without worrying about the potential consequences of a stranger in a customer's home.

11

Safety

Safety is the most important topic in any book about businesses requiring the use of power tools and it's in your best interest to adhere to all safety rules. If you have all your fingers and body parts after years of using power tools, it's probably because you realize the importance of giving every power tool your full and undivided attention before turning it on.

POWER TOOLS ARE INHERENTLY DANGEROUS! Any tool that can cut wood can also cut skin and bone. Please keep this in mind every time you use a power tool. Here are a few simple suggestions that will help you avoid injuries:

- Plan every cut carefully before starting the tool. This is a common oversight. Instead of just jumping in and starting a cut, determine exactly what you are going to do and what problems might be posed by the procedure.
- Another part of planning is to visualize the complete procedure before you start. This will help you avoid potential kickbacks or other injury causing incidents.
- Clamp work pieces securely before cutting, routing or sanding. It is much quicker and easier to just hold the piece down with one hand while making the cut or routing the edge with the other but you are significantly increasing the risk of injury.
- Read and adhere to the safety guidelines that came with the power tool. These guidelines are written to help you avoid serious injuries. It only takes a few minutes to read through the small booklets that come with power tools.
- If you are using a power tool with one hand, always check the location of your other hand before starting the tool.

That may sound silly to some but it is definitely a good way to keep all your fingers. Taking a few moments to do this will ensure that your other hand is in a safe location to avoid possible injury.

- Never use power tools if you are tired, taking medications or using alcohol or drugs. This is a sure way to get hurt.
- Never use a power tool while someone is talking to you or distracting you in any way. It only takes a split second for a serious injury to change your life. If someone interrupts you while using a power tool, stop the tool and tell them it is dangerous to distract you until the tool is turned off.
- Always use ear and eye protection and dust masks while using power tools.

Don't let lack of attention or a moment of carelessness ruin your livelihood and perhaps your life. Think before turning on any power tool and take good care of yourself and others around you.

12

Final Notes

After more than twenty five years of doing almost every kind of home repair and woodworking project, there are few things in these businesses that I have not experienced. I retired from woodworking to write and publish books and this gives me the opportunity to share my first hand experiences. This last chapter contains a few final notes that you may find valuable. In addition to these notes, I welcome hearing from you about your own experiences and any questions that come up for you. Please email me at: bill@positive-imaging.com and I will respond as promptly as possible. Thanks again for purchasing this book.

Become An Expert

To be really profitable it helps to be a recognized expert in your chosen field. People respect experts and are more likely to trust one to do their job. Strive to be the best home repair expert in your area. That's not as difficult as it may seem. Look around and see how many people really excel at their chosen profession. Over the years I've found that most people, including handymen, simply do little more than what is absolutely required. This should make it obvious that all around you mediocrity reigns supreme.

This means that if you simply excel at your work and perform well for all your customers, you will quickly establish a reputation as a highly competent and reliable expert. This also means that people will be willing to pay more for your services because of this reputation.

Develop Your Communication Skills

Those in the top five percent of their field are in demand and are paid the most. What does it take to be in that top five percent? There are two very basic things you must do to attain that status. First, you must have, or take the time to develop, excellent communications skills. That means being able to get your message across clearly to everyone, especially potential customers. Having those skills puts you head and shoulders above most other home repair experts.

If you don't have those skills, work to improve your vocabulary and your communications skills. There are colleges, adult education programs and even home study courses to help you with this. If there is a toastmaster's club near you, join it to improve your rapport with the public.

Are you wondering what this has to do with home repair? Even though it's not directly related to your home repair skills, it has a lot to do with succeeding financially using those skills. Getting people to choose you and even pay you more than others in the field is essential to your success. Good communications skills ensure your message will get across to prospects who will become customers.

Never Stop Learning

The second thing is to learn everything you can about home repair. Never assume that you know everything necessary to succeed in your business. It's not enough to know how to repair a few things. Be prepared for bigger jobs as time progresses.

Learn from every job, from every other handyman, from magazines, from the web, and from the completed work of others. Every time you visit anyone's home keep your eyes and your mind open. See how things were done and determine how you might improve on them. Fill your head with new ideas on how to do things.

Go to trade shows and talk with other handymen. Learn what others are doing and how and why they are doing those things. Find out if those methods will work for you. Perhaps they will serve as the basis for some new methods of your own. Don't just accept existing methods as the end all. Create your own ways of doing things.

Think about how to do things better, faster, easier. Learn how to help your potential customers get the exact job they want or need and how to do it the best way possible. You will have to visualize the project and explain everything clearly to your customers.

Visualize and Share Your Vision With Customers

Don't be from the school that believes you are the expert and the customer doesn't merit explanations. Take the time to explain how you would go about it and why one thing works better than others. If you are from that old school of "I'm the expert and I always know the best way to do things," it's time to get over yourself.

Customers prefer to deal with experts who are willing to explain things even if they don't really understand it all. It gives them a feeling that you value their ideas and desires and they would be better off dealing with you, even if it means paying more than the lower bid. Be an expert who helps people to understand your work and they will flock to you and pay your prices without complaint.

Use Drive Time To Learn

You will probably be driving to various locations to bid jobs and to work on the ones that you get. Instead of spending that time listening to news, music, sports or letting your mind chatter away with useless and often negative messages, listen to motivational messages on your Smartphone or CDs. There are many good ones on the market. Earl Nightingale, who died many years ago, had many excellent books and tapes that are now available as audiobooks. His tape set entitled **Lead The Field,** published in 1972, was my favorite. You can probably get a copy from the Conant Company or at some used bookstore. Try a search on Google to find copies of this great tape set. Such tapes help to instill the values that are important to any one, especially self-employed persons.

Always Go The Extra Mile

Go the extra mile for all your customers. Don't nickel and dime them for small items. Price your work so you don't need to sweat the small stuff. Never make promises that you can't keep. Always deliver what and when you say you will. If a serious problem arises and you can't begin or finish exactly on time, contact your customer as soon as you know about the problem. Don't wait until the last minute and just not show up. Treat all your customers as the most important people in your business because they are.

Be confident and positive with your customers because it builds trust. Never criticize your competition to a potential customer. Sell yourself and your work in a positive manner. If your competitor is doing poor work, his reputation will follow him. Mentioning or dwelling on the poor quality of a competitor's work will give potential customers a negative impression of you and may well cost you a job.

Remember the Golden Rule

Treat customers in the way you would like to be treated. Even though this is simple and the fair thing to do, it's actually quite rare. Most people are simply thinking of their own interest and fail to put themselves in the customer's shoes. If an unpleasant situation arises and you don't know exactly how to respond to it, stop and reflect before you act. This will result in the action that is best for you, your customer, and your business.

Stay Positive

Maintain a positive attitude at all times. Sometimes this is hard to do but it will help you do the best possible job at all times. Know your limitations but be prepared to expand your knowledge to overcome those limitations over time. A positive state of mind will help maintain your health and your business and keep you in that important learning mode. Most people dislike doing business with negative individuals. Fear and doubt can overwhelm almost anyone. Potential customers may sense your doubt and hesitate to contract you for a job.

Remember your love for the freedom of self employment and what a great opportunity it is to make your living doing something you really enjoy. Few people have that unique experience. You can make a good living doing creative and challenging work but don't jump in if you have serious security issues and need a secure income and regular benefits.

Persons with those needs should find a job that offers such security in order to maintain peace of mind. Risk is always a part of self-employment since you no longer have a steady paycheck. Before leaving a regular job to jump into home repair full time, you should enjoy this work enough to accept some risks. If you aren't certain, you can still start on a part time basis until your confidence grows.

Finally, remember that the home repair business is seldom an opportunity to become wealthy. Then again, neither are most jobs, so enjoy your work and good luck.

Covid-19 - The Pandemic

As I write this revised edition, Covid-19 is wreaking havoc with the United States. Some eight million people have contracted it, and some two hundred and fifteen thousand have died from it.

No one knows how long it will be before there is a vaccine. Most of your customers will be concerned about any stranger visiting their home. Acknowledge that concern by wearing a mask and socially distancing. It may be wise even to wear gloves.

No matter how your customers view the pandemic, you must follow the correct protocol to protect yourself and your customers from possible exposure to Covid. If your potential customer has a problem with this behavior, you should avoid that job.

Special Note From Bill

Some of you already have good home repair skills. Others may be good carpenters who know how to install crown moldings and other fine woodwork. If so, use those skills to gradually expand your business into higher paying work.

Learn from the Internet. Google is an invaluable source of information for almost any business. Take the time to search for the kind of information you need for any job. You will find concise and down-to-earth instructions for most home repair tasks. Remember, use it as a source and then apply your creativity to develop original methods.

Use your handyman experiences to learn more about working with wood in other ways. There are many books on woodworking and the woodworking business that can help you to increase your skills, challenge yourself, and make much more money. As you gain those skills, practice them on projects for your own home to make certain that you can do a good job with them. Then practice more on family and friends until you're confident of your skills.

Positive Imaging, LLC offers two paperback book that may help you to learn the skills needed to expand your business into these areas. The title of the one related solely to the business is "**Woodworking Business: Start Quickly and Operate Successfully.**" I know you will find it a valuable book and you can get complete information about it at: http://woodworking-business.com . You can purchase it from that web site or find it at Amazon.com Books.

The second book is geared to building functional pieces for your home or others. The title is **Woodworking Simplified Book 1: Your How-To Guide For Making Attractive and Functional Projects.** It includes complete instructions and drawings for desks, cabinets, bookcases, tables and more. It's another valuable book that you can find at http://woodworking-simplified.com or at Amazon.com Books.

Disclaimer

Everything described in this book is based on my personal experience. Over the years I've gained considerable experience in construction, home repair, and woodworking and am a competent, though not extraordinary, businessperson. Anyone with good skills may be able to attain similar results if he or she puts in the effort. Nevertheless, no guarantees are expressed or implied regarding your own results using the information in this book.

Some individuals are more apt to profit from home repair than others due to the level of their skills, business acumen, and communication ability. Regardless of my experience over the years, I can't guarantee that you will succeed in this or any business.

Business of any kind involves the risk of loss, including, but not necessarily limited to: money, time, and energy. In addition to the financial and time considerations, home repair involves the use of tools that can inflict serious injuries if used carelessly. I have made every effort to accurately describe my experiences in detail, including safety considerations, but cannot be held liable for any damages or injuries that may result from the use of this information–even if the user informs me prior to or after these damages or injuries occur.

The user of this information agrees that he or she is solely responsible for the consequences of such use. It is also the user's responsibility to conduct a reasonable level of due diligence prior to making any business or legal decisions. The information contained and distributed in this book is not intended as nor should it be considered professional, business, or legal advice.

For any questions please contact bill@positive-imaging.com

Glossary

Accounting: a precise record of the financial transactions of your business.

Accounting Software: software used to maintain information on the financial transactions of your business.

Addendum: An addition to a contract to describe additional work or changes to the existing agreement.

Advertising: The activity of attracting public attention to your products or services.

After Market: similar to third party vendors meaning an accessory or attachment made for a tool or product by another manufacturer.

Analyze: to study how best to perform a certain task to maintain safety and avoid injury.

Backlog: home repair projects under contract and awaiting completion for your customers.

Bank Account: a fund at a bank where you can deposit and withdraw funds.

Belt Sander: a power tool that uses a circular belt with an abrasive grit for sanding surfaces smooth.

Billing: The process of sending an invoice to your customers for services rendered.

Capital: funds available to pay the costs of operating a business.

Carbide Tipped: blades and bits that have carbide attached so they will cut more efficiently and remain sharp longer.

Carpenter: a skilled worker who builds, makes, or repairs wooden objects or structures.

Circular Saw: a power saw for cutting wood consisting of a toothed disk rotating at high speed.

Clamps: metal or wooden instruments used to hold wooden parts together while glue dries.

Collection: obtaining payment for your work.

Communication Skills: the ability to convey your point regarding your work clearly and concisely to facilitate selling home repair projects.

Competent: sufficiently qualified to perform the work required.

Complaints: expressions of dissatisfaction with something.

Compressor: a device that compresses air for use with pneumatic tools.

Consumer Tools: tools that are manufactured to lesser standards because of lighter use by non-professionals.

Contract: an agreement between two of more parties to ensure completion of a project and payment for the work.

Creativity: the ability to be original and to develop new ideas using older ideas as a basis or starting point.

Crown Molding: a decorative molding that is applied at the top of a wall, most often against the ceiling.

Customer: an individual or company that purchases your products or services.

Deposit: advance payment collected to ensure full payment on jobs.

Depreciation: a loss in value due to age or wear.

Drawings: line sketches that clearly describe the construction details for a job or project.

Drill: a power tool for drilling holes in wood or metal.

Employee: a person who works for you in return for financial or other compensation.

Expenses: costs associated with running your business.

Expert: a person with a high degree of skill or knowledge on a particular subject.

Finish Sander: a vibrating power sander used for the final sanding on a job.

General Contractor: a person who is responsible for and supervises the activities of those working on a project.

Gross Income: the total income received from your business activities before expenses are deducted.

Hand Tools: tools for various kinds of work that do not require electrical power.

Health Care: the insurance and facilities required to maintain the health of individuals.

Hourly Rate: the amount per hour paid to yourself or employees.

Income Tax: the tax collected by government from every citizen based on the amount of income they make.

Insurance: a contract by a party indemnifying another against a specified loss.

IRS: Internal Revenue Service collects income taxes.

Lacquer Thinner: a liquid used to clean surfaces of lacquer finishes and to thin lacquer.

Learning: the process of acquiring knowledge about certain skills.

License: an authorization from a government body allowing you to perform some form of business.

Maintenance: keeping tools and buildings in good repair.

Materials: products used to repair, build, or make projects or jobs.

Measurements: the dimensions of a specific project used to cut the parts.

Nails: a pointed piece of metal pounded into wood as a fastener.

Net Income: the income left over after all expenses are deducted from the gross income of a business.

Occupational License: an authorization to participate in a certain occupation or business activity.

Online Banking: conducting your banking using the Internet.

Ordinances: laws that apply to various aspects of your work activities.

Overhead: the cost of operating a business.

Paint Thinner: a liquid used to clean or thin oil-based paint.

Payroll: salary paid to individuals for work performed.

Payroll Taxes: taxes deducted from individuals for payment to the IRS.

Penalties: fees charged for not adhering to regulations.

Pneumatic Nailer: a pneumatic tool that drives nails into wood.

Professional: a qualified person engaged in a certain activity for their livelihood.

Profit: what is left after all operating expenses and material costs are deducted from gross income.

Random Orbit Sander: a power sander that rotates and orbits to sand rapidly without creating circular marks on a wood surface.

Reserve Fund: money set aside for one or more specific purposes.

Router: a power tool with a sharp bit used to cut grooves and decorative edges.

Saber Saw: a power saw used to cut curved lines and cutouts in wood.

Safety: steps taken to remain free from danger, risk or injury.

Sanding: the process of smoothing wood in preparation for finishing.

Sanding Belts: circular sanding strips used on belt sanders to sand wood.

Sandpaper: abrasive sheets used to smooth wood surfaces.

Sawhorses: four legged supports to raise work from floor level.

Screws: a metal pin with incised threads used as fasteners.

Security: the idea or concern about being secure and safe.

Self-Employed: working for yourself in a business.

Self-disciplined: being able to perform required tasks without having someone to make certain things are done.

Self-motivated: being a self starter who does not require an external motivating force.

Small Business: varying definitions exist but basically it is a business that is not considered large.

Social Security: a fund that individuals pay into in order to have funds available for retirement.

Specifications: details that describe the specifics of a job or project.

Subcontractor: a self-employed individual who works on a project or job for the individual in charge.

Supply and Demand: the process of setting prices on products based on the demand for them.

Trade Tools: tools manufactured for professionals in various fields.

Visualize: to study the steps involved in doing anything before actually performing the tasks.

Wages: hourly fee paid to employees.

Waste Factor: the amount of material that must be calculated in a job because it will be wasted during the cutting.

About Bill

Beginning at age twelve I spent my summers and weekends working with my dad, a general contractor, building homes and commercial buildings. I contracted to build a house for the first time at age nineteen and built my own home by age twenty. For more than 30 years I operated one-person businesses that included home building, home repairs, cabinetmaking, furniture making, and various other kinds of woodworking activities.

Twelve Years with government programs

Twelve years of my life were spent working for local government administering federally-assisted housing programs. I started as an inspector with a three-month assignment and was Director of Community Improvement with 78 employees when I resigned twelve years later to do writing and consulting. By invitation, I testified on housing issues before the Housing Subcommittee of the United States Congress.

Writing, Publishing and Consulting

For years I operated Rehab Notes Library, my publishing company, publishing a monthly newsletter (Rehab Notes) with subscribers in all 50 states, Canada and England and several books on housing rehabilitation. I also did consulting and public speaking for agencies and organizations in cities across the country. Because of my efforts, several community housing programs developed valuable partnerships with local banks to multiply their federal funding.

My first book on housing was published by the National Association of Housing and Redevelopment Officials. After that I wrote and published eight guidebooks on the subject of housing rehabilitation. In 1980, when federal funding for the housing assistance programs was cut, I took advantage of my construction experience and started my own business doing home repairs and gradually moved into cabinet and furniture making.

Over Twenty Years of Woodworking

For over twenty years, first in Tampa, Florida and then in Austin, Texas, I built hundreds of small and large projects for individuals, companies, churches, and government agencies. During these years I began writing about my experiences.

I published a book and project newsletters on woodworking. My first woodworking book was **Simplified Woodworking I: A Business Guide For Woodworkers.** That was followed by a monthly project newsletter **Simplified Woodworking.** I also performed power tool demonstrations around Texas for the Skil Power Tool Company. After many years of self employment, I encapsulated my self employment experience in my book **The Self Employment Survival Manual: How to Start and Operate a One-Person Business Successfully,** both are now out of print.

Since then I wrote and published **Woodworking Business: Start Quickly and Operate Successfully**. Complete details are available at:

http://woodworking-business.com

Computer Experience

My computer experience dates back more than twenty years. After a couple of bad experiences with on-site technical support, I began working on my own computers. Since then I have taken many courses on computer repairing, upgrading, troubleshooting, building, and networking. I upgraded and built many computers and acquired A+ Certification and MCSE (Microsoft Certified Systems Engineer) Certification.

I was the IT Manager at the Hyatt Regency Austin until January, 2016 when I retired to do writing and publishing full-time.

I was born and raised in Tampa, Florida and moved to Austin, Texas in 1986, where I now live with my wife, Barbara Frances.

Other Books

Other Books Published By Positive Imaging, LLC

Paperback

Woodworking Business:
Start Quickly and Operate Successfully
by A. William Benitez
http://woodworking-business.com

Woodworking Simplified Book 1:
Your How-To Guide for Making
Attractive and Functional Projects
by A. William Benitez
http://woodworking-simplified.com

Biscuit Joiner:
A Woodworker's How-To Guide To Biscuit Joinery
by A. William Benitez
http://biscuitjoiner.woodworking-business.com/

Download A Free Digital Book (ebook)

Woodworking Business
Quick Start Guide
http://free.woodworkbusiness.com/

Additional Resources

For regularly updated information about the handyman business check out our website at: http://home-repair-business.com . Check out this site for valuable how-to information on the same kind of projects you may be doing on your home or in your business. Send us information and pictures about your jobs and they may be included to help others. Send all information to:

bill@positive-imaging.com

A. William Benitez graduated from handyman to full-time woodworker and a much higher income. You can do the same. To learn more about the woodworking business check out our web site at: http://woodworkdoctor.com .

Check out this site for valuable how-to information on woodworking projects and methods to help you learn the business. Send us information and pictures of your woodworking projects and they may appear on the site. Send all information to:

bill@positive-imaging.com

If you have questions about the handyman or woodworking business or about specific projects or methods, please don't hesitate to send them to:

bill@positive-imaging.com

We will do our best to answer them as promptly as possible. Thanks for purchasing this book and we look forward to hearing from you soon.

Made in the USA
Las Vegas, NV
29 December 2024

15560714R00059